IMAGES OF ENGLAND

CREWE

IMAGES OF ENGLAND

CREWE

BRIAN EDGE

TEMPUS

Frontispiece: The miniature railway around the garden of 4, Wellington Villas, Crewe, the home of Mr G.R.S. Darroch. The picture was taken in September 1928. The house is roughly where the car park of Wellington House stands today. Mr Darroch, the Assistant Works Manager, used to drive a blue Bugatti sports car. Many Crewe lads will recall climbing up the wall surrounding this house in an effort to see the railway.

First published 1994
Reprinted 2000
New Edition 2003

Tempus Publishing Limited
The Mill, Brimscombe Port,
Stroud, Gloucestershire, GL5 2QG

British Library Cataloguing in Publication Data.
A catalogue record for this book is available from the British Library.

ISBN 0 7524 3004 1

Typesetting and origination by Tempus Publishing Limited
Printed in Great Britain by Midway Colour Print, Wiltshire

Contents

Acknowledgements   6

Bibliography   6

Introduction   7

one   The Railway Connection   11

two   Around Old Crewe   49

three Sport, Leisure and Special Events   91

four   Wistaston and Haslington   121

       Appendix – Crewe Inns and Hotels   128

Acknowledgements

For the loan of photographs and for sharing their knowledge and happy memories the author would especially like to thank: Philip Barlow, Geoff and Brenda Bavington,
the late Mr A.H. Billington, Mr D. Blackshaw, Miss Renee Bradshaw, Mrs Barbara Brierley, Graham Broad, Jack Bryant, Mr and Mrs J. Clifford, Mrs T. Craven, Mrs Eachus,
Mr and Mrs W.D. Evans, Mr M. Cartwright (Photographer), Mrs Evelyn Clymes,
Howard Curran, Michael Gilsenan, Mrs Mary Hamlin of Ellesmere, Shropshire (for her special kindness), Mr T. Harvey, Peter Healey, Mr and Mrs H.Heap of Wistaston,
June and Peter Howard, the late Albert Hunn, Peter Kirkland, Walter Kirkland, Tom Lockett, Colin and Mary McLean, Mr Arthur Moran, Managing Director, Bowater Security Products (Crewe) Ltd., David Patrick, H.B. Pie, Mr G. Pimlett of the Cheshire Libraries (for permission to use certain material), John Povey, Tom Raiswell, George and Edna Redwood,
Walter and Barbara Sexton, John Schofield, Mrs Edith Scott, Staffordshire Evening Sentinel, Laurie Twiss, Peter Walker, Mrs June Wallace, John Wolstenholme.

Also thanks must be extended to others who have helped along the way and to those who it has not been possible to trace. Sincere apologies are offered to anyone who has not been included in these acknowledgements. Finally it must be explained that in many cases the author has had to rely entirely on contributors for providing the names of individuals featured in these photographs. Apologies are therefore offered to anyone whose name has been spelt incorrectly or who has been wrongly identified.

Bibliography

Challinor, W.H.   *The Social & Economic Development of Crewe 1780-1923*, (Reprint) Augustus M. Kelley, Clifton, New Jersey, U.S.A., 1973.

Eardley, Wilmot.   *Eardley's Crewe Almanack and Diary 1899*, Wilot Eardley, Crewe, 1899.

Porter, Frank.   *Director of Crewe, Middlewich, Nantwich, Sandbach, Northwich, Winsford and District*, Rockliffe Bros., Liverpool, 1889.

Reed, Brian   *Crewe Locomotive Works and its Men*, David & Charles, North Pomfret, Vermont, U.S.A., 1982.

Introduction

Crewe, like many other industrial towns born in the 19th century, has physically changed dramatically over the past 40 years. The way of life of its people has also changed with virtually every aspect of their lives being geared in some way or another to the motor car.

No longer can one say that Crewe is a railway town. The dozens of tall chimneys, which once dominated the skyline have now disappeared, and along with them the jobs which made their existence necessary. So much has happened here since the locomotives Charon and Prince emerged from the paint shop in Crewe Works on the 1st January 1843 (some months before the works was formally opened). Their completion heralded more than a century of work for the town, during which period, officially, 7,331 steam locomotives were to be built. Sadly, the Works (now privately owned), is but a feint shadow of its former glory, when it was accepted as being the most famous railway workshop in the world. So extensive was that establishment in days gone by, that it was possible for a railway employee to get off a train at Crewe Station and via the "Midge" Bridge, walk as far as Merrills Bridge without stepping onto a public road. The hub of the works was the old London and North Western Railway (later L.M.S.R.) General Offices. They were affectionately known to all as "The G.O." but they too have long since closed, the fine building eventually razed to the ground by a disastrous fire.

The 'round the clock' thump of the giant steam hammer in the Works Forge no longer shakes the foundations of the houses in old Crewe town, for both have been swept away and their sites used mainly for car parking. Fortunately, three or four railway built streets in the town centre have been preserved as modern homes, thus giving present generations a rough idea of the style of old Crewe.

The great Victorian chapels which could be found in every part of the town have, by and large, also disappeared, as attitudes towards religion have changed. In those days it was well known that when selecting workers for jobs and in considering candidates for promotion attendance to divine service on Sundays was taken into consideration! These chapels were to have a life span of roughly 100 years, but in their heyday they were so popular that it was often impossible to gain admission on a Sunday night. A story which confirms this tells of a man who carried an urgent message, a matter of life and death in fact, addressed to a member of the congregation of one such chapel. It was only after considerable pleading that the messenger was allowed in, but the sidesman, in granting permission said "Come right out when you have finished, and Heaven help you if I catch you praying"!

The cinema enjoyed similar popularity upon the introduction of talking pictures around 1926. How many readers can recall on a dark, cold and really wet night standing in a slow, shuffling cinema queue? Those who can, will remember those anxious moments when, on nearing the paybox, you were very much aware that at any moment, a purple and gold uniformed commissionaire could thrust a board in front of you bearing the dreaded words "HOUSE FULL!" "Shillings, one and nine and two and three" called the commissionaire as you placed your half-crown on the brass plate where your ticket was to appear almost by magic. Then one would almost run along the corridor and up the soft red carpeted stairs, with their white safety treads,lighted only by the small gas lamps which flickered in their ornamental globes. Eventually a closed door was reached and when opened you were met, first by darkness, then dazzled by the beam of a torch held by an invisible bearer. This you trustingly followed to your seat knowing that you were to sit there for the next two hours in your wet clothes! In front of you flickered the giant screen, the beam of light from the projector struggling desperately to penetrate a dense cloud of cigarette smoke. And then, when quite unexpected, a uniformed usher would walk briskly down the centre aisle carrying a large brass cylinder and from it spraying a questionably fragrant solution into the air. The fallout was eventually received by the entire audience! Many readers will well recognise that experience but they will, nevertheless, still look back on their visits to The Grand, The Kino (Ritz), The Palace, The Plaza (Queen's/Majestic), The Odeon(Focus) and The Empire with considerable nostalgia.

Scores of Public Houses have been demolished as a result of the many changes which have taken place over the years. Thousands of Crewe people have whiled away their leisure hours in those places partaking in a "swift half" – and probably more! A list of Crewe Inns and Hotels appear at the back of this book and some of the defunct establishments can be found illustrated in Chapters One and Two.

Many older readers will remember the old Iron Bridge, the short cut from Forge Street to High Street. One who does, recalls as a child, sitting on the bridge and being fascinated by the rumbling music of the wooden planks as hoards of people crossed from the old town on their way to watch the "Alex" at Gresty Road.

Young people no longer walk the 'Bunny Run' (Market Terrace) on a Sunday night with the hope of being able to 'click'! Modern youth doubtless has the same objective but their methods are somewhat different!

Who remembers having a regular Saturday afternoon stroll down to High Street especially to see the wedding pictures in Bullock's window?

No longer is Chapel Street affectionately known as "Education, Salvation, Condemnation and Damnation" as a result of having a school, a church, a police station and a public house on its four corners, for all but the pub have now disappeared.

Old habits certainly die hard as a few people can still be heard asking for Exchange Street when booking a bus fare, even though, in name, that street has long since disappeared. Fewer, however, will be aware of the location of London Road in Crewe, so, in order to preserve its identity it must be revealed that London Road is the the small passageway off Chester Bridge joining Market Street to Prince Albert Street.

Some will certainly remember the "Four Halls", once the nickname of the junction of Earle Street, Hill Street and Prince Albert Street. It got that name due to the fact that the Cheese Hall was on one corner, the Market Hall on another,on the third corner stood the Town Hall and the fourth, for many years a piece of waste land, was affectionately dubbed the "Beggar 'All", or words to that effect!

John Povey shown here c.1960 alongside his vehicle was 26 years a Refuse Collector in Crewe. In those days, bins had to be carried shoulder high and often for quite long distances. When the bin had been emptied it had to be returned which usually meant four journeys for each bin! During those years John must have, unknowingly, deposited many family heirlooms on the Council tip. Everyone will will recall 'Grandma' saying "Oh! I put them in the bin – only last week", much to the horror of the enquirer. The pictures that you are about to see have, fortunately, escaped such a fate!

A typical scene in Crewe Works in the days of steam locomotion.

Whilst one can still enjoy a game of snooker, older readers will remember "Burtons" Billiards Hall, the "Alexandra"(opposite the Kino) and the Old Billiard Hall off the bottom of Market Street. Some were not the most salubrious of places but nevertheless remembered with much nostalgia by those who patronised them.

Fifty years ago dancing was a most popular activity. Many readers will recall dancing at the Astoria Ballroom; The Town Hall; St Barnabas's Hall; at the Corn Exchange and also above Diamonds on the Terrace. One could Jive at Rattigans Studio in Mill Street and St. Michaels Church Hall was also a very popular venue.

Crewe can still boast of having its own 'real' theatre based on the typical Victorian theatre with pit, circle and gallery. The present theatre, the Lyceum, dates from 1911 and is at present being completely refurbished. When completed it should be one of the towns best attractions. However, the atmosphere of the theatre too has changed along with the town. No longer will the audience roll in their seats when the stand-up comedian mentions a particularly notorious boarding house in the town, or scream with laughter when the same comic confidentially asks if there are any vacancies in the Erecting Shop!

Another activity which lost its considerable popularity as a result of the introduction of Bingo is the Whist Drive. At one time most Workingmens Clubs, Church Halls and Schoolrooms held regular Whist Drives and it was possible to compete for cash prizes on most nights of the week. At Christmas times "Fur and Feather" drives were everywhere and competitors tried their hardest to win their Christmas dinner. In those days it was often a case of no prize - no Christmas dinner.

Whilst on the subject of the festive season Crewe at one time had two Engine Sheds which stabled large numbers of railway locomotives and on New Year's Eve all the steam locomotives would blow their whistles simultaneously at the last stroke of midnight so there was no doubt in the minds of anyone in the town that the New Year had well and truly arrived.

Whilst so much of Crewe above the ground has disappeared it is still possible for the observant to find cast iron sewer covers and grids which are boldly emblazoned Walter Button, Iron Founder, Crewe, which could well be relics of the 19th Century.

Crewe Alexandra's successful season 1993/1994 gained them promotion into the Second Division of the Football League and their success brings to mind a run in the F.A. Cup when they played against Tottenham Hotspur at Whitehart Lane. The tie turned out to be a disaster for the "Alex" for Tottenham won the match by 13 goals to 2. Many special trains of supporters went from Crewe to London on that day and the story goes that one train was late arriving in London and as a result those supporters arrived in the ground after the match had been in progress for some time. One of those supporters found himself a suitable place in the crowd and promptly asked the man next to him if there was any score. "Seven - Nil" was the reply. "Who for" asked the Crewe man hopefully?

Yes, of course that story has been told many times over, but you see, that is nostalgia!

Brian Edge
July 1994

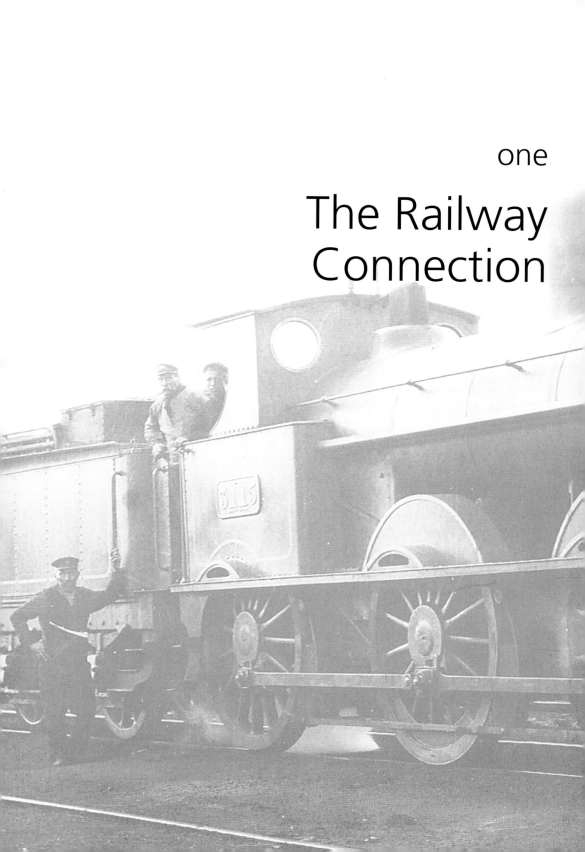

one

The Railway Connection

The Chester and Crewe Railway received its Act of Parliament in 1837 and opened in 1840 only to be taken over by the Grand Junction Railway on the 19th May of that year. The Chester and Crewe Railway had previously acquired land at Crewe for a workshop and the Grand Junction Railway officials saw the possibility of developing and extending this site for their own new workshops. Out of these negotiations came Crewe Works.

Crewe Square in 1897. An Advance Party of reservists parade prior to departure for Aldershot. The idea to establish a Volunteer Corps of Railway Engineers was raised in 1887 by Mr Francis William Webb the Locomotive Superintendant at Crewe Works and Chief Mechanical Engineer of the London & North Western Railway. When the consent of the War Office had been received the proposal was put to the staff employed in Crewe Works and to those employed in other departments of the L.& N.W.R. in the town. There was a remarkable response to the invitation to join the new Corps. Engine drivers, fireman and cleaners, fitters, boilermakers, riveters and smiths, platelayers, shunters and pointsmen all made application and those in charge of recruitment soon found that they had more applications than places available. They were therefore able to select only the best candidates.

Six companies were formed, each containing one hundred officers and men. A. B. C. D. E and F. Companies were commanded by Captains G. Whale, A.M. Thompson, W. Norman, A.G. Hill, H.D. Earl and J.O.B. Tandy respectively, each having a full complement of Officers and N.C.O's. The Chaplain was the Rev. A.H. Webb, and the Medical Officer, Surgeon Major, J. Atkinson, the first Mayor of Crewe. Major L.V. Lloyd, a Director of the L.& N.W.R., formerly of the Grenadier Guards, afterwards of the 2nd Volunteer Battalion, Royal Warwickshire Regiment - became Leiut. Colonel and Officer Commanding. Captain Gossett, R.E. was appointed Adjutant, Sergeant Goss, R.E. was instructor and Sergeant-Major to the Corps, and Corporal Staig R.E. was the second instructor. The above picture shows the Reservists in uniform at Blackpool in July 1898. Note the "pillbox" style hats.

The men won a reputation for smartness. Indeed they were commended for their appearance and for the efficient way they performed their duties by the Duke of Cambridge, the Commander in Chief of the Army. The Duke inspected the Guard of Honour which was provided by the men of the Corps on the 4th of July 1887. This was on the occasion of the opening of the Queen's Park, which was a gift from the London & North Western Railway to the town. The picture shows the Corps Band at Rhyl in 1895.

A sporting young lady in 1897 resplendent in uniform jacket and the early pillbox hat. Exactly who Sapper "Poppie" was we may never know, but we do know that there were no ladies in the Battalion! Her willingness to dress up as she did has left us with an excellent photographic record of the uniform particularly the facing locomotives on the collar. The locomotive depicted is the 3000th steam engine to be built in the Crewe Locomotive Works. It was considered that the Battalion was the best equipped, armed and accoutred body of volunteers in the country, all ranks were replete with three suits of clothing, namely - scarlet tunic, scarlet frock, blue frock, blue greatcoat, helmet, peaked cap, and field cap.

At Rhyl during Whitsuntide 1889 the Crewe Railway Volunteer Engineers got practice in track laying. Note the narrow gauge track they used for moving materials.

Whilst at camp in Rhyl in 1895 they built this 105 feet span trestle railway bridge. Such skills were the speciality of the Crewe Works "Army".

The Bugle Band at Rhyl in 1897.

On the Rifle Range at Holmes Chapel in 1895. The reservists had an excellent drill hall, drill field (complete with locomotive), a rifle range and all the equipment to train the six companies. In addition the raising of this Battalion from the employees of one organisation was unique, it being the first instance of such, anywhere in the world.

Marching off to the Boer War on the 16th October 1899 and what a send off! Can anyone imagine that so many people, for any reason, will gather in Mill Street again? The picture gives a rare view of the George and Dragon which closed its doors in the first decade of this century.

The whole Battalion had volunteered and stood by for South Africa. However, they were not all required to go. The Special Railway Reservists attached to the Corps at Crewe were called up together with two detachments of volunteers. In total 285 officers and men went to South Africa. They were engaged there driving armoured trains, building bridges and blockhouses and putting up wire fences. Twenty six Crewe men died in the conflict, 19 of disease, 3 by accident and just four killed by the Boers. The names of all these men are recorded on the South African War Memorial in Queen's Park. The Battalion was called the 2nd Cheshire Royal Engineers (Railway Volunteers).

A section of the 2nd Cheshire R.E. band c.1905.

The Drum Major gives advice to a young bugler in 1897.

Another excellent study of the reservists' uniform, taken at camp in 1907. His first name was George. Upon the creation of the Territorial force in 1908 the Crewe Engineers became the Cheshire R.E. (Railway Battalion) Territorial Force and were commanded by Colonel H.R.L. Howard. They were eventually disbanded in March 1912.

Crewe Station, Number 2 Platform, August 1899. An excellent study of gleaming L.& N.W.R. locomotive Number 1920 – "Flying Fox" (Jubilee Class) about to depart with an express passenger train. A lone member of the platform staff patiently awaits the "right away" from the guard. (Note the very old style milk kits which stand on the next platform). These compound locomotives were built between 1897 and 1900, and along with other "compounds" were generally erratic and unreliable. Although they pulled well uphill they were sluggish on the level and often had to be double headed, even with light loads. This led to much ridicule of F.W. Webb's "compound policy" and as he cured one problem, another appeared. The unreliabilty of these locomotives certainly had much to do with Webb's downfall and retirement from the post of Chief Mechanical Engineer Crewe Works in 1903.

This locomotive shown working on the Malines-Terneuzen Railway in Belgium was originally a Crewe built, London & North Western Railway, D.X. Class goods loco. (Built some time between 1858 and 1874). At the time the picture was taken c.1906 it still carried its Crewe number plate 3115.

Another early Crewe built engine. A 2-2-2 SFB tender loco shown here c.1906 under repair or possibly under conversion at St Nicholas Works on the Malines-Terneuzen Railway in Belgium.

Accident at the Cumberland Bridge, Crewe, March 18th 1905. Spectators watch the steam crane which has come to the aid of the stricken locomotive. The 0-6-0 assisting engine is numbered 1270.

The Saddlers Shop Football Team c.1910.

The Crewe Works Fire Brigade in 1910. The Fire Brigade was called out by three long blasts on the works hooter. The Fire Brigade Train was kept under Chester Bridge. Two of the firemen in the picture are wearing medals.

Crewe Railway Works Fire Brigade c.1960. The officers in the centre of the picture left to right are: Captain Rodden, Chief Inspector Hanley, and Sub Captain Jackson.

The Crewe Railway Works Fire Station c.1960 showing the engines and pump.

Mr T. Morgan is depicted at his desk in the General Offices of the London & North Western Railway, Chester Bridge, Crewe c.1900.

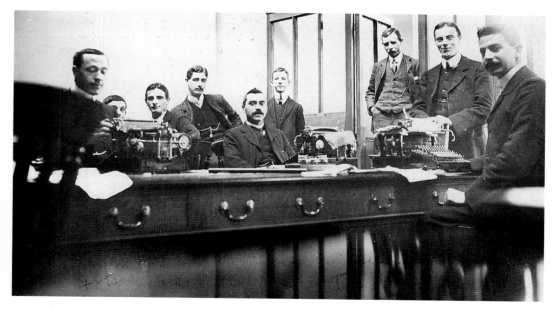

The Correspondence Room in the L.& N.W.R. General Offices about 1906. Left to right in the picture. E. Sephton, H. Gibson, Geo. Gibson, A. Challinor, F. Billington, F. Thomasson, Alf Bott, Tom Wood. Note the three ancient typewriters on the desk.

The London & North Western Railway Mechanics Institute more or less occupied the triangle bounded by Earle, Prince Albert and Liverpool Streets. This picture shows the interior of a part of the building.

The bar and staff at the Mechanics Institute, c.1909.

Librarians in the Mechanics Institute Library about the time of the First World War.

This Crewe man was a Gas Meter Inspector for the London & North Western Railway prior to World War 1. At this time the Gas Supply was owned by the Railway company and even the domestic gas stoves in the town bore a plate marked "Property of the L.& N.W.R." A rare picture of a rare grade of railwayman.

First World War Memorial in Crewe Works. The Memorial was erected by the employees of the Fitting Shop (Steelworks) and Fitting Shop(old Works). It records that 92 men (Steelworks) and 185 men (Old works) joined the forces and fought for the liberty of mankind. The following made the supreme sacrifice.Steelworks: J.C. Arrowsmith, A. Cartwright, S.L. Dunne, F. Gater, A. Higginson, A.L.Hudson, W.A. Newton, C. Nightingale, H. Platt. Old Works: A. Beresford, H. Brownsword, H.W. Farrington, S.K. Mapp, C. Neild, L.H. Oldham, F.R. Parker, A. Perkins, W.B. Rogerson, J.W. Rylance, R.L. Symon, P.C. Stearns, F.N. Tassell, J. Thompson, C.P.C. Vance, and C.D.M. White. The memorial now stands along with others in the Machine Shop Arcade.

Albert Sutton at work lifting a 60-foot railing out of the furnace in Crewe Works new steel plant in 1927.

Crewe Station.

"THE FARE'S 21/6, CHANGE
AT CREWE."
"IF YOU DON'T MIND, MON,
I'LL HAVE MY CHANGE
NOW."

Above: Platform Four at Crewe Station as it was c.1930. The photo shows an orderly platform with clear directional signs for passengers. The picture is taken from a picture postcard posted in November 1931 which bore the message: "This is where the lady got out of the train who wanted to go to Birmingham – she is still here – I've just seen her !!"

Left: There have been many changes since this 1940 postcard was designed. Booking Offices (with origins in the days of the Stage Coach) have, in name, disappeared. Third Class subsequently became Second Class and in more recent years has become Standard Class! Money has been decimalised and both the shilling(bob) and sixpence(tanner) have been demonitised. The humour, however, remains good!

L.& N.W.R. Royal Train approaching Crewe 5th May 1904.

THE ROYAL TRAIN
EN ROUTE

A letterheading as supplied to the London Midland and Scottish Railway Royal Train.

Euston Station, London, 15th October 1926. Nine Crewe Royal Train Drivers are being presented to King George V and Queen Mary. In the picture Queen Mary speaks to Alfred Eachus. The men were: Alfred Eachus (age 74; 58 years service; 5,100 Royal Train miles); William Jefferies (72; 51; 3,380); William Hughes (77; 56; 3,268); Samuel Galley (71; 56 1/2; 1,200); J. Tansley Hollins (72; 55; 1,200); John Ford (76; 52; 1,200); John Jones (72; 50; 1,200); Sampson Wright (76; 55; 750); Alfred Elson (73; 54; 600); These drivers remained in service until 70 years of age and between them clocked up 20,460,000 miles without a single accident. So remarkable was their record it was the King's special wish that he should be able to meet them and congratulate them. As he shook each man by the hand the King said "I'm proud of you".

Few people have done more to enhance the name of Crewe than Tom Clark who, at the time of his death in 1954, lived in Bedford Street. Tom, shown here with his fireman, had just completed record runs on Crewe built locomotive 6201 Princess Elizabeth in 1936. Tom was destined to set another record and on Tuesday 29th June 1937, just a year before he was due to retire, he drove faster than any man had previously driven a train in Britain. Tom drove 6220 "Coronation" from Crewe to Euston a distance of 158.1 miles in 2 hours 9¾ minutes. He returned the same day in 1 hour 59 minutes breaking the record in both directions. At one point on the return journey he and his fireman achieved the speed of 114 m.p.h between Whitmore and Crewe. During this famous run R.A. Riddles, the Engineer who was in charge of the test, and on the footplate delayed the braking when approaching Crewe in order to attain the record speed. This action almost caused a disaster at South Junction but the streamlined train did stop short of any obstruction and fortunately all turned out well in the end. Tom was also a Royal Train Driver and in 1937 he drove King George VI and Queen Elizabeth, The Queen Mother(Queen Mary), The Princesses Elizabeth and Margaret from Carlisle to London after one of their trips to Scotland. At Euston the King sent for Tom, who in his overalls, cap and oily hands went along to the Royal Coaches where the King conferred upon him the Order of the British Empire.

A London & North Western Railway train approaches Crewe Station from the north c.1904. The old Crewe North Signalbox can be seen in the centre of the picture and on the left is the 18" tramway suspension bridge (220 ft main span) known as the "Spider"or "Midge" Bridge. This was used by pedestrians after the Frst World War.

Crewe North Junction Signalbox c.1939 showing the Spider(Midge) Bridge in the course of demolition. The picture shows the men at work and the Lookoutman watching for their safety.

The building on the right is Crewe North Junction Signalbox in 1940 which was nearing the end of its useful life. It had been in use since about 1906. The foundations for a new concrete signalbox can be seen. The new box, together with its partner at Crewe South Junction, were to be built to withstand enemy bombing. Fortunately they were never put to the test. In the distance wagons stencilled G.W. and L.M.S can be seen, behind which is the large loco coaling plant which was in the vicinity of Lockett Street.

Crewe North Junction Box complete after the old brick built box had been demolished. The box was brought into use over a number of days beginning at 5.00 a.m. on Sunday the 25th August 1940.

The interior of the new Crewe North Junction signalbox with duty signalman. The box remained in use until being replaced by Crewe Signalling Centre in 1985.

The interior of Crewe South Junction Box which was brought into use over a number of days beginning 4.30 a.m. on Sunday the 29th September 1940.

Dad's Army! A group of Crewe Home Guard c.1940 in front of a Stanier Black Five (one of the most popular locos of the L.M.& S.R.). The photograph seems to have been taken on the Vacuum Pits outside the Brass Finishing Shop in the Works.

Opposite above: An embarrassing situation for somebody! A freight train is derailed at Crewe North Junction about 40 years ago. Crewe North box can be seen on the right...

Opposite below: ...and it took the big steam crane to sort things out!

Above: The L.M.& S.R. Sports Club Dramatic Society's presentation of Noel Coward's 'This Happy Breed' in the the Work's Canteen, Goddard Street on Friday 11th April 1947. The cast left to right were: Margaret Jolly, Irene Elks, Albert Barber, Wilf Edwards, Douglas Bimson, Dilys Edwards, Betty Dudley, Bob Warhurst, and Janet Fleet. The society originally produced their plays in the old Corn Exchange, but eventually made their home at Goddard Street, which had an enormous stage with excellent facilities for the artistes. They produced about three plays a year until the society wound up about 1969.

Right: Renee Bradshaw gives Dougie Bimson a piece of her mind in a L.M.R. Dramatic Society production.

The L.M.R. Sports Club Dramatic Society presentation of Esther McCracken's 'No Medals' was given on the 27th October 1948. Left to right: Peter Grahl, Wilf Edwards, Jimmy Flood, Hilda Moses, Renee Bradshaw, Dilys Edwards and Margaret Jolly.

The London Midland & Scottish Railway's E.R.O. (Executive Research Office) Stationery Store in Bridle Road. This was to become British Railway's Paper and Printing Division until July 1989 when the complex closed. This view of the "Locked Stock" area, taken on the 9th October 1945, will be familiar to hundreds of Crewe men and women who worked in the store during its lifespan of nearly half a century. Miss Eileen Powell (now Mrs Dyer) and Miss Renee Bradshaw are featured in the picture.

The Bessemer Hotel, Richard Moon Street was opened on the 11th October 1874 by Mr H.F Winby. The establishment took the place of a former Bessemer Vaults which had stood in Bessemer Street, upon which site the Steelworks was erected. The pub was a facility for the workers in the nearby melting furnaces and casting pits where the workers were allocated a beer ration and 'Beer Lads' were employed by the Railway Company to carry the ale from the pub to the works. For this purpose The Bessemer, a Greenhall Whitley's house, at one time had a 24 hour licence. The historic pub, really a part of Crewe Works, was demolished without ceremony c.1980.

The last British Railways Standard Class 9F (2-10-0) to be built in Crewe in December 1958. The engine was to be numbered 92250 and was, officially, the 7,331st engine to be built in the works. In the picture l.to r. Peter Walker, Tom Davies and Jimmy Wilkinson.

Opposite above: Crewe Locomotive Works 'Deviation' Gate which once stood at the end of Eaton Street. The Work's Fire Station can be seen just to the left of the Gatekeeper's head. The notices forbid cycling within the works.

Opposite below: Engine 41272 an Ivatt L.M.S. design 2-6-2 Tank is seen leaving the Paint Shop amid great jubilations. The engine bears plates on the side of the tanks which read "This is the Seven Thousandth Locomotive built at Crewe Works, September 1950".

1950 Crewe Works Inter-Shop Cup final at Goddard Street Ground. General Offices Team. Back row, players only, left to right: Harry Bingle, John Churchill, Charlie Cauldwell, Eddie Teggin, Norman Payne, Les Mills, Ken Fleet. Front row: Horace Blackburn, Herbert Jones, Frank Foster, Tom Raiswell. Mr Forsythe the Works Manager is seated in the centre of the picture.

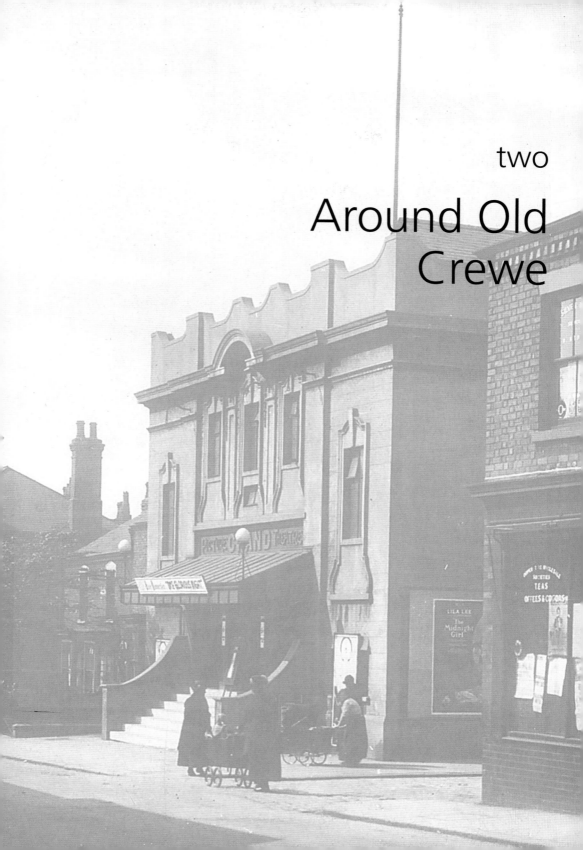

two

Around Old Crewe

Above: Nantwich Road outside the Royal Hotel as it was in the 1920's. Daimler bus registration number FM 1385 approaches. The parked car on the right bears the numberplate FY 7899. The dog in the picture is waiting for the bar to open! The metal sign above the door was issued by the Automobile Association and reads CREWE – Nantwich 4 Sandbach 6, London 165 – SAFETY FIRST.

Left: A terraced dwelling in Pedley Street, long since demolished.

Only three of the gables shown in this picture of Market Terrace survive today. The whole character has changed since the picture was taken just before the First World War. The shops include Hilton and Hilton and Battams. Signs refer to Pianos, Cycles (10/- per month) and Furniture. There is also a bar which advertises Radcliffes Arizona Beer!

Market Street c.1938. Wallace Wainwright's shop is on the right with offices of the Royal Insurance Company above. In the centre is S & H Morris's wholesale and retail Wallpaper Warehouse (Agents for Walpumur, Duradio, and Vesta Paints). The first vehicle has an LG licence plate. There have been extensive changes to the right hand side of the road but apart from the sun-blinds, which are now bygones, and the cobbled road, the left hand side is much the same today.

Market Street Crewe in 1904. Shops comprise a herbalist, tobacconist, hairdressing saloons (2), and Hamiltons the practical tailor at number 65. The white building on the corner of Victoria Street is the Grand Junction Hotel and the cupola caps the Co-operative Buildings.

View from a corner of Wellington Square in 1957. (Wellington Square stood somewhere between Wellington House and the back of the new Doctors surgery on Victoria Street).

Right: Outside number 22 Charles Street Crewe c.1910. Charles Street occupied the site of the Bus Station today and comprised typical houses built for railway workers.

Opposite below: Crewe Market Square c.1904. The General Post Office was architecturally a very fine building. The Odeon Cinema (Focus) eventually occupied this site before it, too, was demolished to make way for the present shops and new Post Office. The old Crewe-type houses on the right stood approximatively where Delemere House car park is today.

Liverpool Street 1961. The motor car creeping into the picture is a Flying Standard.

Church Street in 1961. Church Street along with Moss Street and Moss Square were cottages built by the railway company. Before demolition they stood behind Christ Church.

Earle Street c.1905 taken from Boots' corner. One can see R.C. Hill's (Wine and Spirit Merchants) Agents for Dix & Company Ltd., Celebrated Ales and Stout. Next door is the Clothing Hall, then Russell and Andress (Chemist), A.F. Hawthorne (High Class Grocer), J.R. Kilner, The Cheese Hall Hotel, the Market Hall and Municipal Buildings in the course of construction.

The corner of Bridge Street and Hungerford Road in 1964. These houses were demolished and the road extended to form Macon Way.

Heathfield Avenue c.1910 looking in the direction of Hightown, not a motor vehicle in sight!

Alexandra Street in 1961 a year before the street was pulled down. The name above the shop door is E. Gayton.

West Street, Crewe

The Grand Theatre, West Street. The playbill reads "The Midnight Girl", a silent picture, starring Lila Lee a demure American leading lady of the twenties. The shop on the right of the cinema was a Cooperative Store. The signs advertise tea, coffee and cocoa.

Oak Street in December 1952, taken from a point now occupied by the roundabout. All the buildings and the chimney shown have now been demolished except for the "Duke of Bridgewater" public house which can be seen in the far distance behind the telegraph pole.

Flag Lane from Alton Street showing the playground c.1930. Obviously a most popular spot. The land behind the playground was to be the site of the Crewe Public Swimming Baths which were completed in 1937.

Opposite below: Number 36 Park Huts October 1951. After the First World War, to relieve the housing shortage in the area, 69 second-hand army huts were erected on ground opposite the main entrance to Queen's Park. The commencing rent was 12/6d per week. The 'Huts' which were to be used as a temporary measure were not to be demolished for 40 years!

Wistaston Road c.1907. The pub on the corner of Flag Lane is the Earl of Chester, the sign reading "Wilderspool Sparkling Ales – the Greatest Wines, Spirits and Cigars – Good Stabling". Walkers Whisky is also advertised. On the right is Johnsons the Wistaston Road Post Office. The sign on the shop on the opposite corner reads "Meat Store". In the distance Edward S. Woolf's Brewery can be seen.

St.Michael's View 1967.

This old army hut was opened in 1920 as the Sydney Workingmens Club. It was eventually demolished in 1961 and replaced by a then modern building and car park.

The Victoria Inn in Victoria Street as it was c.1890. Whilst the establishment still exists it is hardly recognisable from this photo.

The Engine Inn on the corner of Mill Street and Station Street. It was an Ind Coope house and when this picture was taken a delivery was taking place. Note the wooden barrels which have long since become bygones. The pub originally was called the Steam Engine and on the 12th of October 1869 the landlord, Mr A. Giblin, hosted the 27th Annual Meeting of the Crewe and Coppenhall Association for the Prosecution of Felons. A body which was eventually taken over by the introduction of Magistrates' Courts.

The Lord Nelson, Mill Street, specialised in Wilsons Ales.

The Railway Inn on the corner of Station Street and Wesley Street. This pub was a Walker's House.

The Queen's Hotel, Station Street sold Ind Coope's Ales. The picture shows the Landlord standing in the doorway.

Clark's Grand Bazaar at the Corn Exchange prior to 1899. In Eardley's Guide of that year the following advert appears: "The Original Great Anglo American Bazaar Company, 33, High Street and 2 Hill Street, Late of the Corn Exchange and 49 Victoria Street. Open daily 9 a.m. to 9 p.m. 50,000 useful and ornamental articles all at one price - 6 Qw d. We Baffle Imitators!"

Edward Rainbow Hill's store on the corner of Edleston Road and Union Street c.1895. Hill almost drove the Crewe Co-operative Society out of business 100 years ago when, coupled with a severe depression he accumulated a chain of eighteen shops in Crewe and district.

Hill's store on the corner of Wistaston Road and Flag Lane c.1895. It is now a general store. Whilst Hill's business enterprise put great pressure on the Co-operative Stores it was to be his business that eventually succumbed about the turn of the century.

The corner of Middlewich Street and Henry Street c.1895. The shop is now a Newsagent. Edward Rainbow Hill served on the Crewe Council for nearly a quarter of a century and became the Father of the Council. He was never Mayor as he claimed that he could not afford it!

Hill's grocery store on the Nantwich Road corner of Edwards Street c.1895. The shop is now a travel agency. Hill was such a popular character in the town that they named a street after him. Not Hill Street (as this already existed) but Rainbow Street.

George Sutton was in business as a shoe repairer in Earle Street. During the Second World War the shop was badly damaged by enemy bombing and closed down soon afterwards. The picture was taken about 1927 and the poster in the window advertises a thanksgiving service at Bradfield Road Chapel and also the current showings in two cinemas, the Queen's (High Street) and the Palace (Edleston Road). One of the films advertised is "Private Izzy Murphy" an American silent film made in 1926.

The Crewe Co-operative Friendly Society Limited West Street Branch (opposite the Park Gates Entrance to Crewe Works) c.1910.

W. Consterdine's butchers shop on the corner of Alton Street and Walthall Street about the time of the First World War. The building is almost unrecognisable today but the small wall on the right of the picture and the decorative support around the doorway above it remains unchanged.

Smethurst and Holden's Shirt Factory in Queen Street c.1920. The North Ward childrens playground is in the foreground.

Interior of the Shirt Factory – a Christmas c.1950.

Cumberland Wharf c.1929. Crewe had many coal merchants who were based at either Thomas Street or the Cumberland Wharf which was at the end of Middlewich Street - now a sports track. The vehicle is a Ford "T" and was bought in 1927 from Ward's Garage in Hightown. Ted Robinson and Raymond Bavington are shown in the picture with their personalised railway wagon which travelled between Crewe and the North Staffordshire Mines bringing in the popular "Holly Lane" coal.

Mill Street Primitive Methodist Church c.1905.

Beech Street Free Christian (Unitarian) Church. (Opened 1865). The pub sign which has crept into the picture reads 'The Rifleman'.

The Wedgewood Primitive Methodist Church faced the Lyceum Theatre in Heath Street. It opened in 1865 when it replaced the the previous place of worship Heath Street Hall which had opened in 1855. The site is now part of the open air market.

The Church of England Missionary Society Soldiers and Sailors Rest and Refreshment Rooms c.1916. This building was situated where the Nantwich Road block of Rail House stands today. Many readers will recognise the small hut at the left of the picture as the Privilege Ticket Booking Office where for many years railway employees obtained their travel concessions.

This establishment was used by vast numbers of servicemen in both world wars who needed to while away the hours between connections. Many hundreds of Crewe people worked voluntarily in this building and many lasting friendships with the servicemen were made. These pictures were taken by Wilmot Eardley in the early part of the First World War after the formation of the Royal Flying Corps but before the formation of the R.A.F. The R.F.C was part of the Army which explains the omission of Airmen from the name of the establishment.

The Games and Leisure Room. A piano, billiards table, draughts, dominoes, cards and writing facilities were available.

The Dormitory. This was heated by a large stove in the centre of the room. At least a dozen clean beds were available. One would surmise that it was summer time when the picture was taken as only one blanket was supplied per bed. As the occupants would need to go for trains at all hours, a clock was also provided. The only sign in the room forbids smoking!

The Nantwich and Crewe Motor Bus Companies first open topped motor bus registration M 878. The bus came into service on the 15th July 1905. There seems to be no shortage of passengers!

Opposite above: Public transport in the 1920's. A Daimler Bus Number 7 (Registration Number FM 703) is depicted together with its crew in uniform. The sign on the front of the bus reads 'CREWE via SHAVINGTON' and the boards on the side read 'NANTWICH, CREWE, SANDBACH, MIDDLEWICH.' Note the solid rubber tyres.

Opposite below: A fine array of Bedford Coaches c.1950 owned and operated by Roberts Coaches Ltd. who had offices in Market Street. The firm was eventually taken over by Salopia Coaches of Whitchurch.

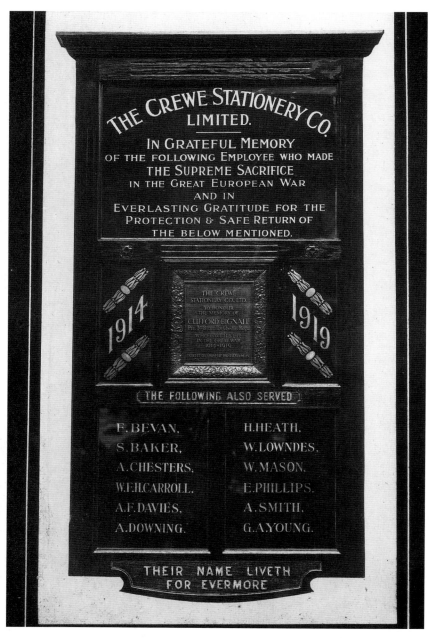

THE CREWE STATIONERY CO.
LIMITED.

IN GRATEFUL MEMORY
OF THE FOLLOWING EMPLOYEE WHO MADE
THE SUPREME SACRIFICE
IN THE GREAT EUROPEAN WAR
AND IN
EVERLASTING GRATITUDE FOR THE
PROTECTION & SAFE RETURN OF
THE BELOW MENTIONED.

1914   1919

THE CREWE
STATIONERY CO. LTD.
TO HONOUR
THE MEMORY OF
CLIFFORD BIGNALL
Pte. 3rd Battn. The Cheshire Regt.
WHO GAVE HIS LIFE
IN THE GREAT WAR
1914-1919

THE FOLLOWING ALSO SERVED

F. BEVAN,   H. HEATH,
S. BAKER,   W. LOWNDES,
A. CHESTERS,   W. MASON,
W.F.H. CARROLL,   E. PHILLIPS,
A.F. DAVIES,   A. SMITH,
A. DOWNING.   G.A. YOUNG.

THEIR NAME LIVETH
FOR EVERMORE

The Crewe Stationery Company Ltd., Francis Street, Crewe, has been generally known in more recent times as "McCorquodales". It is, however, now properly called Bowater Security Products (Crewe) Ltd. The picture shows a memorial plaque to Clifford Bignall of the 3rd Battn. of the Cheshire Regiment, a warehouseman for the Crewe Stationery Company Ltd.. Clifford had served six years with the company before his call up in August 1914. He was killed in France on the 17th February 1917. The memorial shows the names of twelve other members of the staff who served in the Great War: F. Bevan, S. Baker, A. Chesters, W.F.H. Carroll, A.F. Davies, A. Downing, H. Heath, W. Lowndes, W. Mason, E. Phillips, A. Smith and G.A. Young. The actual whereabouts of the memorial plaque is unknown.

The Ursuline Convent c.1910 which today houses the Cheshire Constabulary Training Centre and Maintenance Headquarters.

The Kindergarten in the Ursuline Convent c.1918. No doubt these types of desks will be familiar to many older readers!

St. Paul's Infants School Class 2 c.1909. The school was on Hightown.

Adelaide Street School Knitting Class c.1911. The girls are working on four needles, probably knitting socks.

Bedford Street School Medal Winners c.1912. These smart and well kitted out lads had a tough time ahead with the Great War looming.

Adelaide Street School c.1914. The girl on the extreme left of the front row is Bertha Hill and Rose Harvey is third from the right on the front row.

The girls of St. Paul's Junior school c.1920.

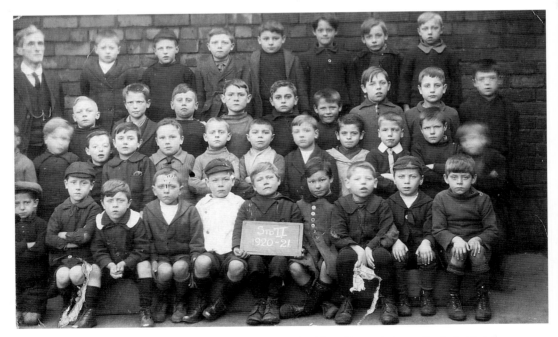

The lads of Standard Two Adelaide Street School 1920-1921. Tom Harvey is immediately behind the boy in the white coat. No doubt many of these boys served in the Second World War.

Borough Senior School Boys (Brierley Street) – Party commemorating the Coronation of King George
VI and Queen Elizabeth in 1937.

The girls of Ludford Street School in March 1935. These girls are shown reviving the craft of Pillow Lacemaking after the lapse of a generation. The photograph shows the girls making the pillows. After these have been covered, a pattern is affixed to the pillow and pins are inserted according to the pattern. Then bobbins of cotton are woven around the pins and the lace is formed. The finished product was used for trimming petticoats, hankerchiefs etc.

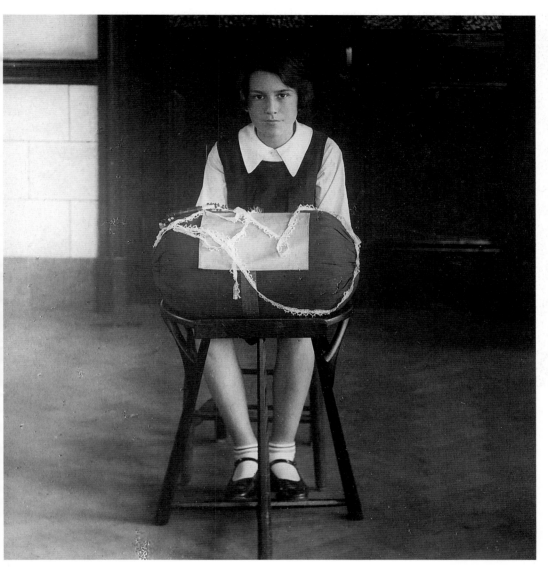

The Pillow Lace made by the girls at Ludfor d Street School Crewe was exhibited at the World's Educational Congress at Oxford from the 10th to the 17th of August 1935. The picture shows Miss Renee Bradshaw, Age 12, with her pillow and samples of the lace that she had made.

Crewe County Secondary School Football Team 1943-4. Back row left to right: Mr Hodgkison,
A. Parks, B. Lockyer, P. Wainwright, Mr Phillips. Middle row: J. Lovell, R. Eaglesfield, B. Norgain,
R. Marshall, J. Clifford. front row: A. Cooke, R. Turner and S. Davies.

Crewe County Grammar School Cricket Team c.1945. Back row left to right: Mr Hodgkison,
B. Thompson, B.Lockyer, B. Norgain, G. Entwistle, Mr. Phillips. Middle row: J. Green, A. Cooke,
J. Clifford, J. Negus, R. Marshall. Front fow: I. Hannah, G. Clifford, R. Eaglesfield.

Crewe County Grammar School Hockey Team 1946. Back row left to right: Miss Slee, M. Williams, M. Rosson, B. Newton, Miss Smith. Middle row: M. Bell, B. Thorley, E. Challinor, M. Pirie, M. Edwards. Front row: B. Thompson, S. Price, H. Palmer.

Crewe Grammar School, 3rd Year Team, 1947. Back row left to right: Mr Dowling (Headmaster), Bob Simmons, Peter Young, John Palin, Mr Walker, Mr Phillips. Middle row: Arthur Horton, Brian Preston, Ralph Benson, Tom Raiswell, Dave Hill. Front row: Dave Looker, Horace Wakeley, Brian Capper.

Crewe Schoolboys Team 1947. Cheshire Schools Shield Winners. Back row left to right: Mr Wilkinson, Mr Mason, John Palin, Arthur Horton, Peter Young, Bob Simmons, Mr Brooks, Mr Jones. Middle row: Ralph Benson, Tom Raiswell, Derek Makin, Eric Speed, George Reeves. Front row: Ben Brierley, Joe Marks, Frank Blunstone (with ball), Stan Jackson, Tony Johnson.

Ludford Street Secondary Modern School, Woodworking Class c.1951. Left to right: Andrews, Michael Orme, Bill Davenport, Norman Bennett, Wilf Walton, John Schofield, Tony Makin,-?- , Graham Broad, Norman Dodd, Rodney Maddocks, Keith Metcalf, Ronald Bourne. The Woodwork teachers were Mr Barlow and Mr Negus.

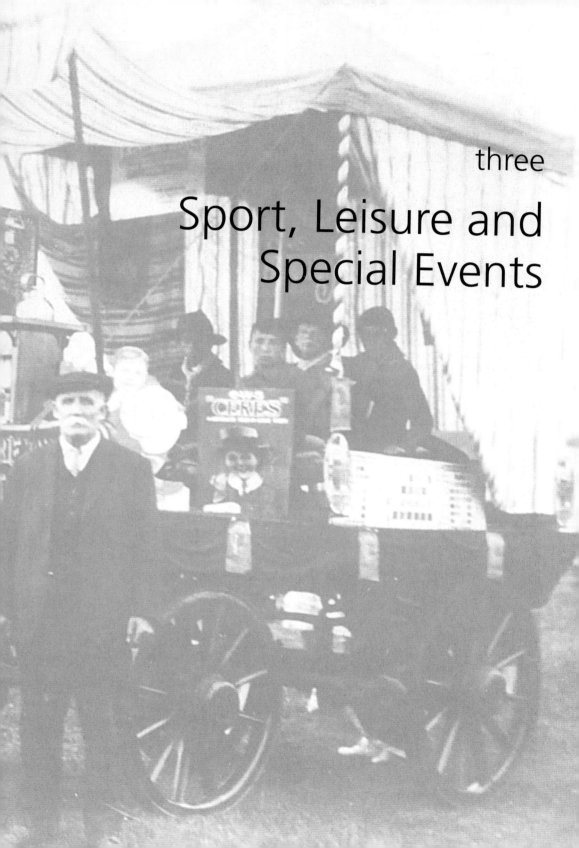

three

Sport, Leisure and Special Events

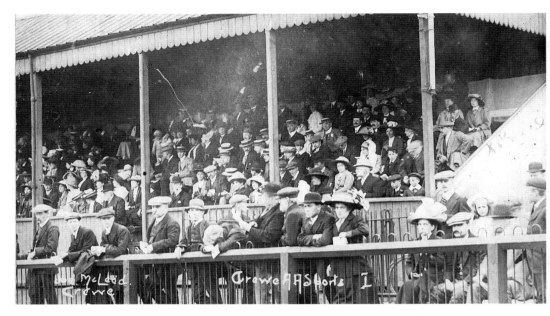

Fashions in the Grandstand at the Crewe Alexandra Athletic Sports in 1912. Over the years many great stars competed at the athletic stadium around which at one time was a banked cycling track where cycling stars like Reg Harris appeared. Cricket and Speedway Racing followed with Barry Meeks setting a world speed record. More recently Stock Cars and Banger Racing were featured. The stadium has now closed.

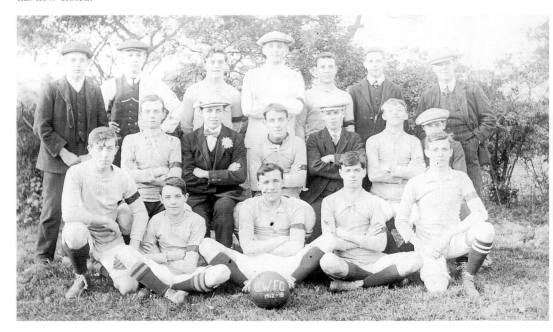

Coppenhall Wesleyan Football Club 1912-1913. Those identified are: Back row: Colclough, Alcock, Ralph Shaw, Atwood, Lightfoot, Mason, -?-. Sitting: Parsons, Morris, George Barnett, -?-, -?-, -?-. Front Row: Tom Evans, -?-, Frank Gadd, -?-, -?-.

Coppenhall United Football Club 1919-1920 Season. Back row: Mitchell, -?-, Jack Hulse, J. Walker, A. Lloyd, Roberts, Raymond Bavington, The Hart Brothers. Middle row: L. Collyer, C. Mason, F.Heathcote Front row: -?-, T. Prince, -?-, G. Jacks, J. Webb.

Popular Crewe Boxer Jackie Potts c.1925. Jackie lived in Elizabeth Street and was in later life well known as the landlord of the Leopard Hotel in Nantwich.

Crewe Villa 1946–1947.

Crewe Alexandra 'B' Team 1949/1950. Manager: Howard Reay. Trainer: Howard Maden. Local players included: Eric Speed, Tom Raiswell, Alan Baldwin, Alf Dixon, Jack Sinclair and Frank Blunstone. Frank Blunstone played for Crewe Alexandra, transferred to Chelsea and subsequently played for England.

The Mayor's procession enters the Municipal Buildings for the Opening Ceremony in 1905.

Crewe Salvation Army Band in 1906. The band conductor is W.B. Garratt.

The Crewe May Queen 1906. Miss Ida Windsor of Alton Street.

Miss Ida Windsor of 116, Alton Street, Age 12. The Crewe May Queen 1906, in her Coach, hauled by four white horses with postillions. The coach and horses were loaned for the occasion by Ward Brothers. Miss Windsor's Maids of Honour were: Misses Amy Lowe, Amelia Fuller, Betty Mansfield, Annie Ellis, Annie Lloyd and Kathleen Brennan. The buildings in the background are the backs of Wistaston Road.

Miss Ida Windsor, the retiring Crewe May Queen on the 29th May 1907. The picture was taken in Alton Street and the Bowling Green of the Hop Pole Hotel can be seen in the background.

The Crewe May Queen, 1907. Miss Nina Capper.

Pioneer Aviator Gustav Hamel c.1912 along with the Mayor and local dignitaries in front of his Bleriot monoplane somewhere in Crewe (possibly where the King George V playing fields are today).

This bonfire was built between Denver Avenue and Clifton Avenue in the first few years of the century but the actual occasion is uncertain. Whilst every care was taken in its construction as can be seen from the photograph, the pile was declared to be unsafe by the police and was never lighted. The picture was taken by C.J. Windsor a professional photographer of 116, Alton Street.

There are 28 'Guys' on this celebration bonfire in 1911. Each is wearing a commemorative medal issued on the occasion of the Coronation of King George V and Queen Mary. Situated on a cinder mound the bonfire was lit by the Mayoress using a taper held in a silver holder which had been presented to her by Councillor Clement Fox. The railway sleepers which make up the bonfire must represent a forest of trees.

The Crewe Cottage Hospital Fete Procession passing over Chester Bridge on August 11th 1906. The shops of Edwin Booth (Chemist and Seedsman) and Wilmot Eardley (Printer) can be clearly seen, with the wall of the General Office in the distance. Everybody clearly joined in the carnival spirit in those days. Note the unusual stretcher which is intended to be propelled by two cyclists.

A busy scene on Market Street outside the Blue Cap Dog public house on Carnival Day c.1911. A policeman restrains a youth from getting involved with the wheels of Lyne's Bread Van.

Crewe Carnival Procession c.1910. This troupe of Frenchmen was made up of staff from the L.N.W.R. General Offices.

Some members of the troupe were: top row: Edgar Billington, Harry Godfrey, Tom Mansfield, Tom Wood, Arthur Evanson, Fred Roscoe, Dick Coen , -?-, Jack Platt, -?-, Colin Cooke.

'American Barbers on Strike' was the title of this troupe made up of the staff of 5 & 6 Erecting Shop in Crewe Works about the time of the First World War.

Crewe Co-operative Friendly Society's decorated float presumably for the Crewe Carnival. c.1911.

The North Steam Shed's Troupe of Japanese Fan Dancers together with their officials in 1924.

Another great North Steam Sheds carnival troupe c.1925 shown here in their blue velvet costumes. There was always great competition between the North Sheds and the South Sheds at carnival time. Sitting third from the left on the fourth row is Harold Clymes, a popular Crewe musician. Laying in the front of the picture is Laurence Rattigan the groups' choreographer. Many readers will remember Laurence's dance studio in Mill Street.

Crewe Carnival procession c.1906. A band comprising many unusual musical instruments passes the shops of Strangward and Plumb (Bakers- Hovis Bread being advertised), G.R. Ball, 49, Nantwich Road, (shop to let) and Philip Platt (Ladies Mantles and Costumiers).

Six lovely Crewe girls in real carnival spirit about the time of the First World War. Back row: Stubbs, Southern, Lapworth. Front row: Tarry, Williams and Williamson. Three of the girls hold a cigarette but they are all unlit and the manner in which they are being held would indicate that none of the girls were smokers!

"The Sleeping Beauty."

WEE GEORGE WOOD, Boy Comedian and Mimic.
The Smallest Artiste on the Stage.

GIPSY'S P.M. CONCERTS HENRY STREET

On New Year's Day, 1915, H.M.S. "Formidable" was sunk in the English Channel by a torpedo from a German Submarine. Amongst those who lost their lives were two Sick Berth Attendants :

JOHN & HENRY RUSSELL,
(twin brothers).

Their bodies were washed ashore and brought to Crewe, their native town, for interment. As they had kindred ambition and inclinations in life and were rarely seen apart, the following lines were written and dedicated to their memory ;—

TOGETHER they first saw the light of day,
  Together at mother's breast they lay,
Together they smiled, together they cooed,
Together they settled their childish feud,
Together they toddled the self-same way,
Together they progressed day by day,
Together at school they learned to spell,
To reason, and think, and do all things well ;
Together they worked, together they played, [ed,
By life's cares and worries they were ne'er dismay-
Together they joined the Ambulance Corp,
Together they studied and came to the fore ;
Together they answered their country's call,
To secure for us victory or 'neath our flag fall,
Together they suffered, together they died,
Together embraced, brought home by the tide ;
Together they traced their oft' beaten track,
Enshrouded in glory and our Union Jack,
Together by father they now lie at rest,
Numbered we know with those of the blest.

                      H.A.H.

Above: A scene from a concert held in Henry Street Primitive Methodist Chapel c.1905. The chapel opened in 1880 prior to which services were held in John Rigg's factory nearby.

Above left: Claimed to be the smallest artiste on the stage, Wee Georgie Wood appeared at the Lyceum Theatre Crewe from Monday the 4th November 1907 for six nights and a matinee in this presentation of the "Sleeping Beauty" or The Prince with the Golden Key. He continued to tread the boards until he was advanced in years.

Left: The Russell twins managed to get into a lifeboat, but died of exposure after 24 hours at sea. Their bodies were thrown overboard but were eventually washed ashore at Lyme Regis. The bodies of the men were brought back to Crewe by train and thousands of people lined the streets to see the cortege pass. They were buried in Coppenhall Churchyard. Two other Crewe men died in the same disaster.

An assembly on the stage in the Crewe Town Hall on the 15th March 1911 who were presenting a cantato entitled "The Fishing Fleet".

Whilst no prizes are offered, have fun, play the age old game by completing the limerick! A 1927 comic postcard.

The Grand Finale of what seems to have been a great show at the Crewe Town Hall in 1932.

And from the same show Vince Schofield with a troupe of glamourous dancers.

"The Quaints" a very smart and popular Crewe dance band c.1930. Left to right in the picture : Edgar Harrison, Sid Garrett (who also played in Foden's famous Band), Bessie Buckley (Singer), Harry Cliffe (drums), Big Hal Clynes, ?.Dickinson (piano), Sid Johnson (Sax) and Cliff Phillips. These boys were real musicians having 18 instruments between the seven of them. Picture taken at either the Borough School or the Lyceum Theatre.

Another shot of "The Quaints" dance band. This set 'on board the S.S. Hearty' was specially built for the extremely popular New Years Eve "Conversazione" which was held in the Technical School at the end of Richard Moon Street during the 1930's. The musicians from left to right: Sid Garrett, Harold Clynes, Cliff Phillips, Harry Cliffe, Bill Crimes and Noel Murray.

Alan Cliffe, another popular local drummer in the 1950's.

Crewe St. Peter's Scouts in 1915. The Boy Scout Movement was only seven years old at the time.

Crewe St Peter's Boy Scouts 1915. The boy on the front right is William Howard.

Crewe Auxillary Fire Service. Trophy Winners c.1936. The photo was taken outside the old fire station in Beech Street. Back row second from the left John Healey.

CREWE CORPORATION FIRE BRIGADE, Prizes Won in the year 1938.

These are the prizes won by the Crewe Corporation Fire Brigade in 1938.

Rolls Royce Crewe on the 29th December 1940 when a lone German Bomber scored a direct hit on the factory.

This is the crater made by the bomb.

Christ Church Choir in 1949. Front row starting fourth from the left: Mr Owen, Mr Curtis, Reverend G. John and Mr Kellson the Organist. The choir boy on the front row second from the right is Peter Healey.

Infantry Workshops R.E.M.E. (Territorials) at camp at Aldershot in 1963. These were Crewe men and they did their "square bashing" on the Catholic Bank (where Kwik Save Supermarket stands today).

Arthur Street Crewe and its residents celebrating the 25 years reign of King George V and Queen Mary in 1935.

Arthur Street and residents enjoyed the Silver Jubilee Celebrations so much that they made an all out effort to decorate their street for the Coronation of King George VI and Queen Elizabeth two years later and as a result won first prize for the best decorated street.

A typical Crewe street party with the viands on display.

A suitable caption for this might be "Will you take that picture quick so that we can get stuck in!"

Queen Street Coronation Day Party – 1953. This celebration was held in the old Crosville Club which at that time stood about where the Post Office Telephone Exchange stands today.

This Crewe Street had its own unique interpretation of "Neighbourhood Watch".

Queen Elizabeth II on the Square at Crewe on Wednesday the 2nd November 1955. The Queen was accompanied by the Duke of Edinburgh for this Royal Visit. The Royal Salute was given by the Guard of Honour of the Cheshire Yeomanry under the command of Major G.V. Churton. The Odeon Cinema, demolished some years ago, can be seen in the background.

Princess Margaret shaking hands with George Eardley V.C.. On the 16th October 1944 at Overloon in Holland, Acting-Sergeant George Eardley of the King's Shropshire Light Infantry and his platoon faced an enemy machine gun post which was generating fire so intense that it seemed impossible for any man to expose himself and remain unscathed. Notwithstanding this, Sergeant Eardley moved forward with sten gun and grenades and knocked out the post. Almost immediately another machine gun opened up spraying the area with fire and in response Eardley charged over 30 yards of open ground to silence the enemy gunners. Then another machine gun post opened up and this time Eardley instructed his men to lie down whilst he crawled forward alone to deal with the occupants of the post with a grenade. His outstanding initiative and magnificent bravery resulted in him being awarded the Victoria Cross. Mr Eardley worked for many years as a maintenance electrician at Rolls Royce, Crewe.

four

Wistaston and Haslington

Church Lane, Wistaston c.1910 from about what is now the junction of Sandylands Park. Without the assistance of the church the scene would be unrecognisable today. One wonders who are the young ladies in the picture?

Old cottages in Wistaston which have long since been demolished. They were located virtually opposite number 61 Church Lane close to Wistaston School.

Number 61 Church Lane can be seen on the left of the picture. The house remains but the thatch has long since been removed. The old cottages shown in the previous picture are opposite. The horse and trap together with its top-hatted driver can be seen on many pictures contemporary with this period. It seems that this was the local taxi in those days!

View in 1920 of what is now the junction of Church Lane and Park Drive taken from the old footpath. The stump of the large tree still remains for all to see in the corner of the garden of 108, Church Lane. The picture is almost beyond belief today.

Crewe Road, Wistaston looking in the direction of Crewe Railway Station. The area being known as Garden City. When this picture was taken one could freely cycle on the wrong side of the road although you would doubtless be prosecuted if caught by the local "Bobby"! The first house on the left is number 577.

The Wistaston Memorial Hall as it looked many years ago. The building was opened in 1949 with funds raised from door to door collections and receipts from special functions organised by dedicated members of the local community. The Hall is a memorial to all local men who fell in battle in the 1939-45 War. A memorial plaque is situated above the main entrance to the hall and this is illuminated by an ever burning light.

Wells Green c.1960. The Wells Green Branch of the Crewe Co-operative Friendly Society Limited closed its doors for the last time over 25 years ago and the building is now known as Brooklands House, a Joint Practice and Medical Centre.

Crewe Green Avenue c.1906 before the road was made up and when the horse and cart ruled!

Crewe Green Cottage. Winner of the First Prize in the Haslington Show's Flower Garden Competition in 1906.

St. Matthews Church Haslington (rebuilt in 1810). The view shows how the church looked in 1910 since when further alterations have been made to the building.

Main Road, Haslington c.1905 approaching the Dingle in the direction of Sandbach. The old black & white cottage has long since been demolished.

The Fox Inn Haslington as it was c.1890. The sign over the door reads "Charles Horton Licenced to sell Wines and Spirits, Ale, Porter, Tobacco Etc". Frank Porter's Directory of 1889 shows Ellen Horton as licenced victualler at "The Fox".

The Fox Inn, Haslington c.1938. The sign advertises the Birkenhead Brewery Company's "Peerless" Ales, Stout, Wines and Spirits. The pub is much changed today.

Crewe Inns and Hotels

This trip around the pubs of Crewe will no doubt jog the memory of many readers and as a result prompt much interesting discussion. The list shows pubs located within the boundaries of Crewe during the past 120 years or so. Over half of pubs on the list have now disappeared. All the main establishments are shown, but no doubt there were also many "Beer Houses", perhaps just the front room of a dwelling, which are not shown here. Those that are known however, have been included. In cases where an establishment is located on the corner of two streets it has been attributed to the most obvious address and where there may be some doubt both streets are given.

Alton Street: Rockwood Inn (The Dog). Beech Street: Beech Tree, Rifleman. Bessemer Street: Bessemer Vaults. Bradford Road: Merlin. Broad Street: Black Horse, Bridge Inn, Spring Tavern. Brookhouse Drive: Raven. Church Yard Side: Bluebell. Dewes Street: Raven. Earle Street: Belle Vue, Borough Arms (Potter's), Cheese Hall Vaults, Crown Inn, Foresters Arms, King's Arms Hotel, Little Crown, Market Arms (Tavern), New Inn, Old Vaults (Pig and Whistle), Rising Sun, Vine Hotel. Eaton Street: Forge. Edleston Road: Duke of Bridgewater, Imperial Hotel. Flag Lane: Old Vine Inn. Ford Lane: White Lion. Heath Street/Hill Street: Castle. High Street/Chester Bridge: Commercial. High Street: Jubilee Tavern, Old Vaults (Kettels). High-Town: Chelwode Arms. Jubilee Gardens (Rear of): Greyhound. Landsdowne Road: Flying Lady. Lockett Street (Bank Street): Cannon Inn. Ludford Street: Spread Eagle. Market Street/Earle Street: Adelphi. Market Street: Blue Cap Dog, Grand Junction, Masonic Inn, Nag's Head, Red Bull Hotel. Middlewich Street: Cumberland Arms. Mill Street: Albion Inn, Anchor Inn, Duke of Wellington, Engine Inn (Steam Engine), Express Hotel, Globe Inn, George and Dragon, Lord Nelson, Neptune Inn, Ram's Head, Royal Oak Hotel. Nantwich Road: British Lion (The Pig), Brunswick Hotel, Crewe Arms, Earl Of Crewe, Egerton Arms (The Barrel), Robin Hood Inn, Royal Hotel. North Street: Horse Shoe. Oak Street: Bee Hive, Oak Farm and Cyclists Hotel. Oakley Street/Albert Street: Albert Hotel. Pedley Street: Unicorn. Plane Tree Drive: Royal Scot. Pyms Lane: Ash Bank. Remer Street: Cross Keys. Richard Moon Street: Bessemer Hotel. Stafford Street: Harp, Vernon Arms. Station Street: Queen's Hotel, Railway Inn, Stirling Tap. Sydney Road: Hunters Lodge, Sydney Arms. Thomas Street: Comfortable Gill, Laburnum Inn, Lord Raglan Inn. Underwood Lane: Captain Webb, Delamere Arms (The Blazer). Victoria Street: Angel Hotel, Burton, Staffordshire Knot, Star Hotel, Swan Hotel (Big Duck), Union Inn, Victoria Inn (Bitter End). Warmingham Road: White Lion. West Street: Brunel Arms, Bull's Head, The George Inn, Lion and Swan Hotel, Prince of Wales, Talbot Inn, Wolverton Arms (The Monkey). Wistaston Road: Earl of Chester Inn, Hop Pole Inn, Island Green, Queen's Park Hotel, Stag Inn.